I0484622

Bringing a Picture to Life

The Seven Elements of Art

Written & Background Illustrations by

Katie Madison

Character Illustrations by

Giuliana Devivo

Copyright © 2017 Katie Madison.

All rights reserved. No part of this book may be used or reproduced by any means, graphic, electronic, or mechanical, including photocopying, recording, taping or by any information storage retrieval system without the written permission of the author except in the case of brief quotations embodied in critical articles and reviews.

Balboa Press books may be ordered through booksellers or by contacting

Balboa Press
A Division of Hay House
1663 Liberty Drive
Bloomington, IN 47403
www.balboapress.com
1 (877) 407-4847

Because of the dynamic nature of the Internet, any web addresses or links contained in this book may have changed since publication and may no longer be valid. The views expressed in this work are solely those of the author and do not necessarily reflect the views of the publisher, and the publisher hereby disclaims any responsibility for them.

Any people depicted in stock imagery provided by Thinkstock are models, and such images are being used for illustrative purposes only.
Certain stock imagery © Thinkstock

ISBN: 978-1-5043-7246-6 (sc)
ISBN: 978-1-5043-7247-3 (e)

Library of Congress Control Number: 2016921539

Print information available on the last page.

Balboa Press rev. date: 12/30/2017

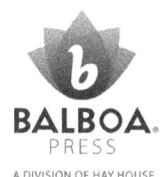

BALBOA
PRESS
A DIVISION OF HAY HOUSE

For Zach and Maddie. Chase the dreams you have deep in your heart... believe faithfully... you will catch those dreams!

XOXO

In this story, Courageous Kate and Super Joe sent themselves on an artistic assignment. To create a picture of their most favorite destination — one that is like looking through a window to a beautiful place. Their special place has an ocean and beautiful plants and lots, and lots of sand. Can you guess where this area might be?

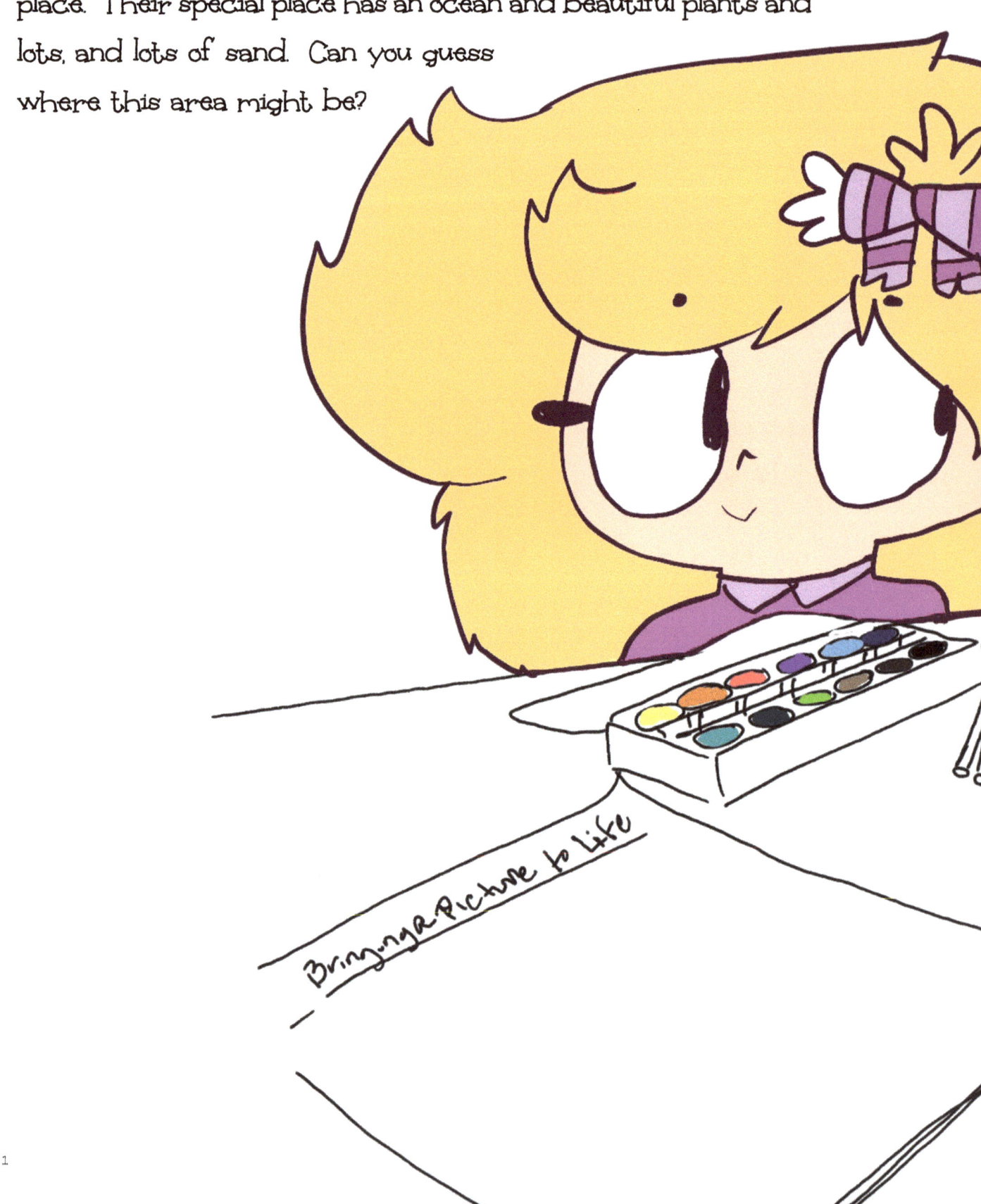

Bringing a Picture to Life

"How do we begin?" Super Joe asked Courageous Kate. Courageous Kate answered, "If we use the seven elements of art to create our picture, we will have our favorite place. And in case you didn't know, the seven elements are the building blocks of art. With those we can put together any picture." "Awesome..." said Super Joe.

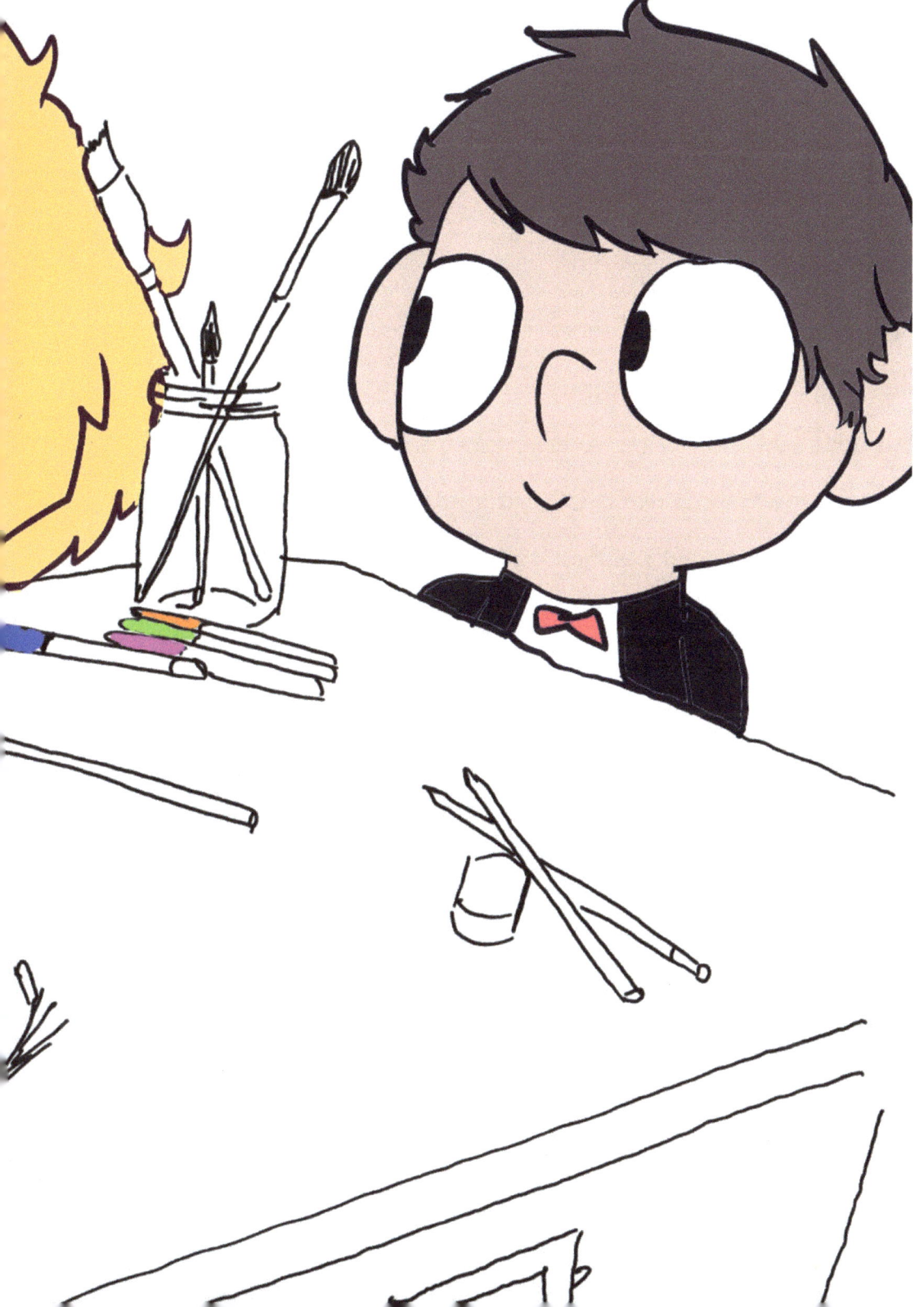

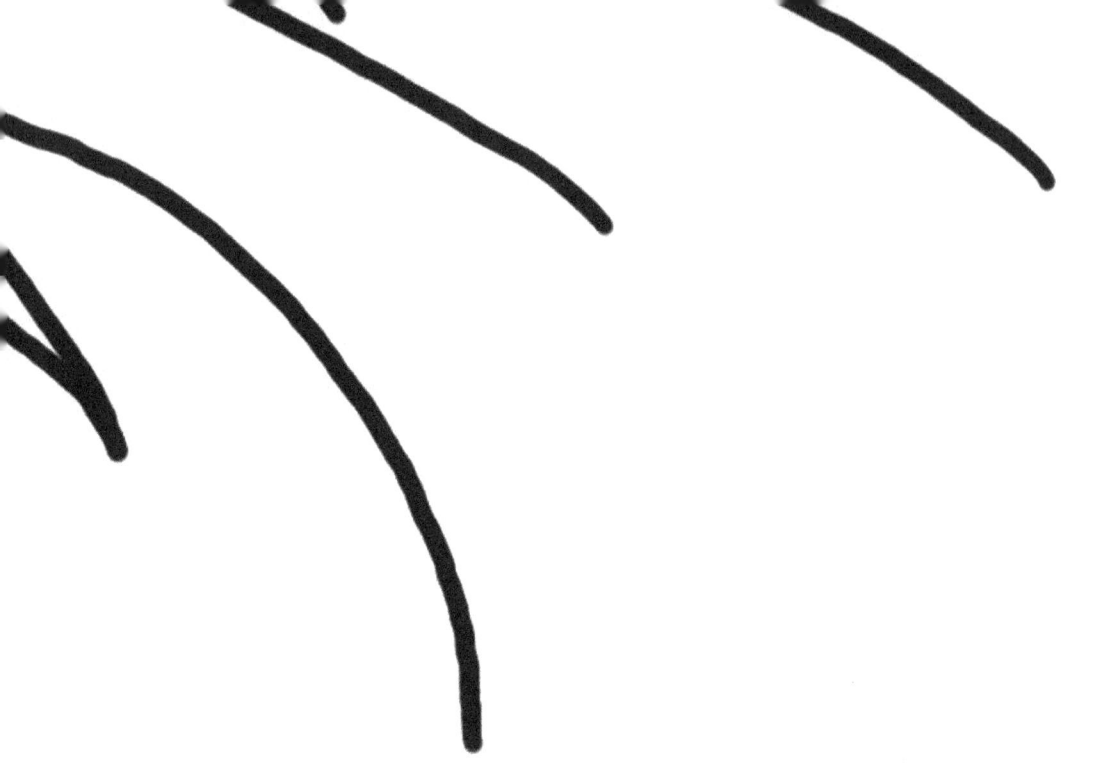

"Let's start with a pencil, paper and turn a dot into a **line**," said Courageous Kate. So, Super Joe began with a dot, and with a stroke of his pencil, turned his dot into a line. Courageous Kate said, "Joe, some lines also go up, down, and even curve around, some are thick, and others are thin. A few lines are dashed, and some are dotted. Others twirl, curl, and zigzag around!"

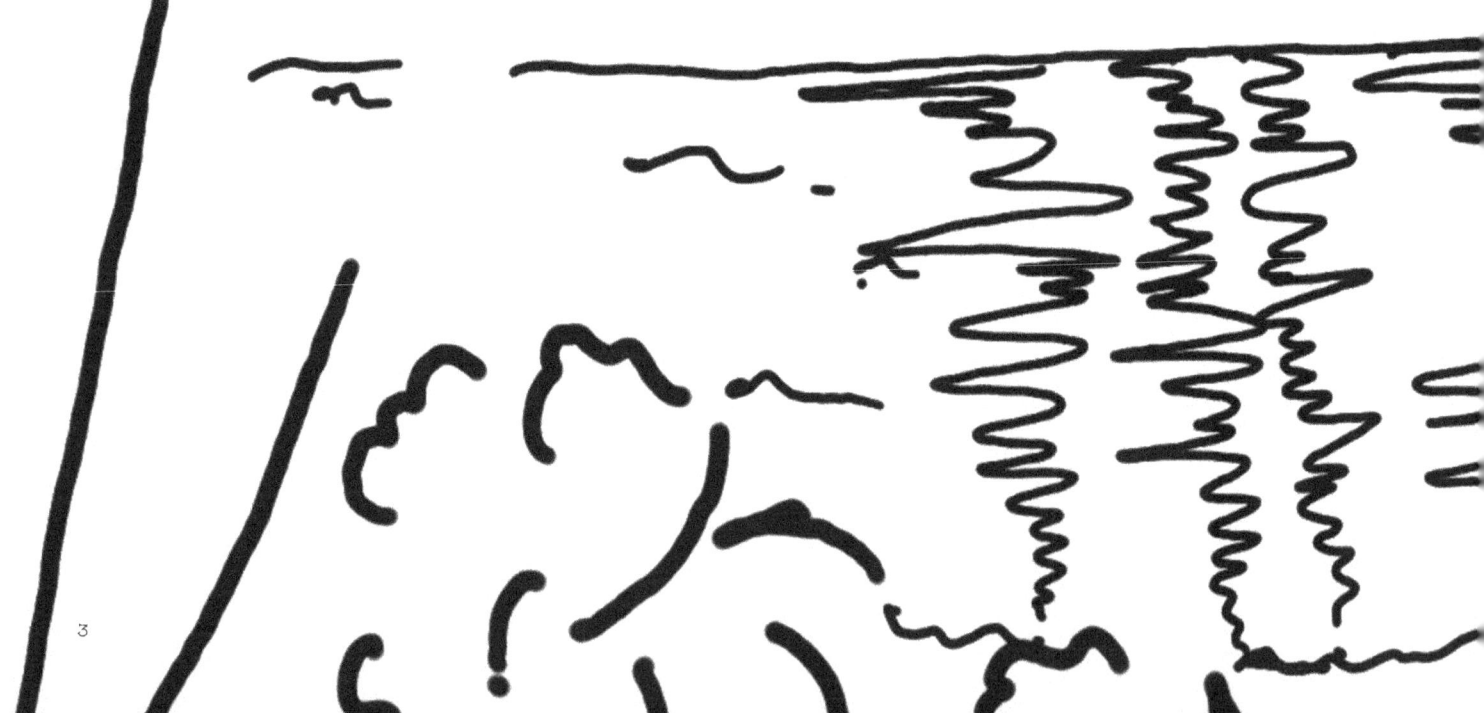

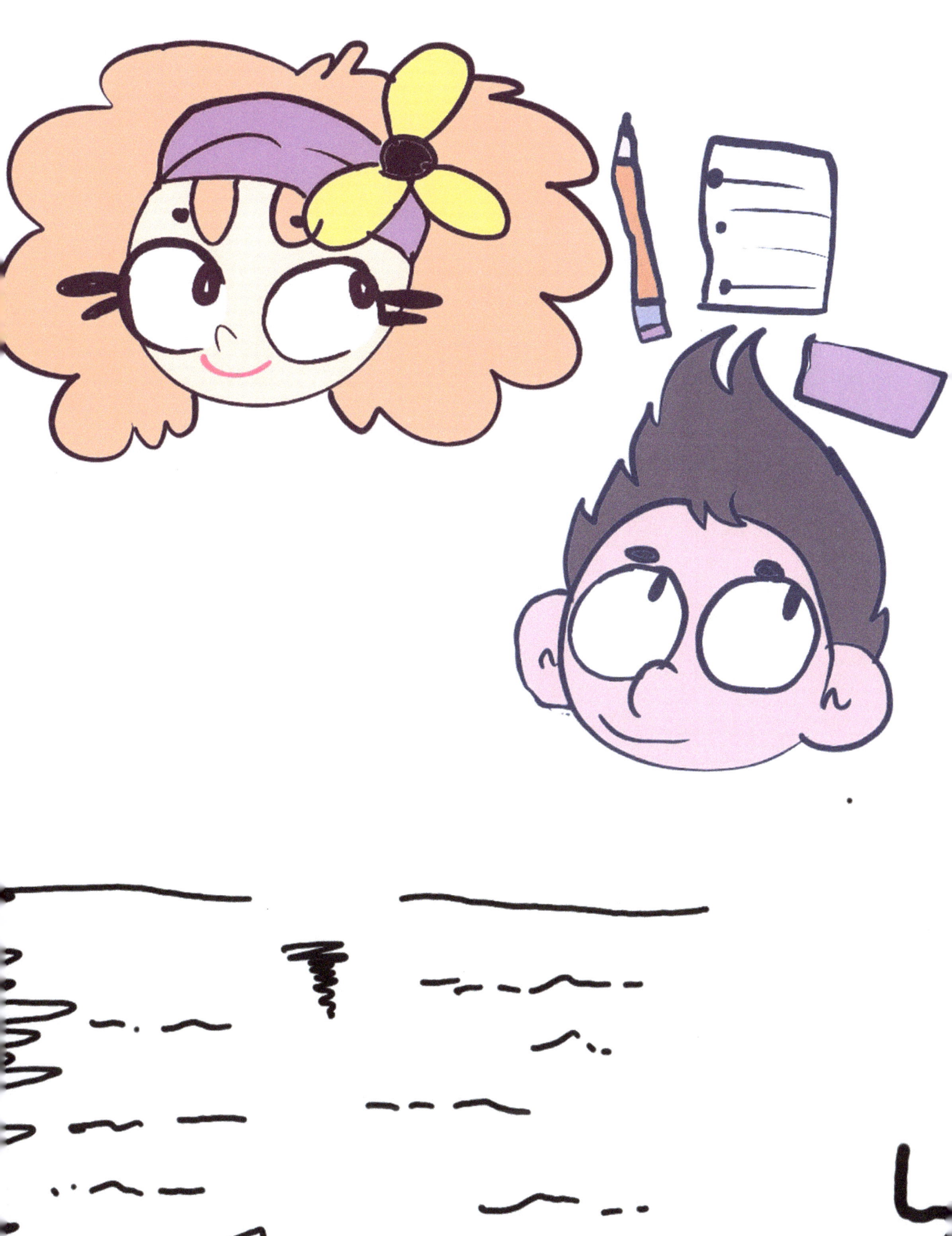

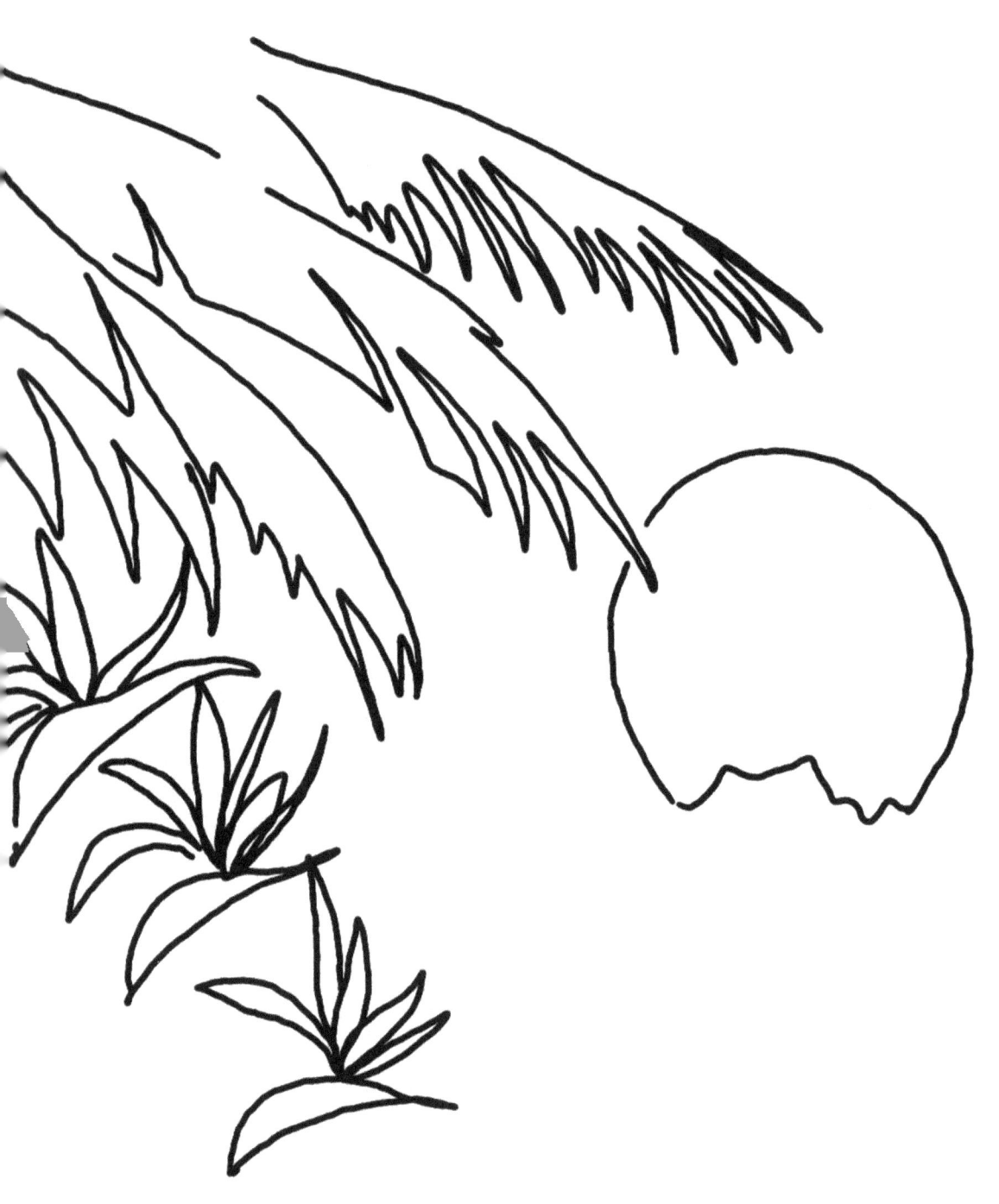

"Look, Kate," said Super Joe. "Some of our lines have overlapped!" "Oh my!" said Courageous Kate, "we've created **shapes**! Shapes are lines that meet together."

So Super Joe decided to add shapes with straight lines and corners called geometric shapes. Then he created shapes with curves and round sides called organic shapes. Courageous Kate noticed and said, "Joe, those organic shapes look like something in nature, and the geometric shapes you drew look like shapes in math." "Awesome," said Super Joe.

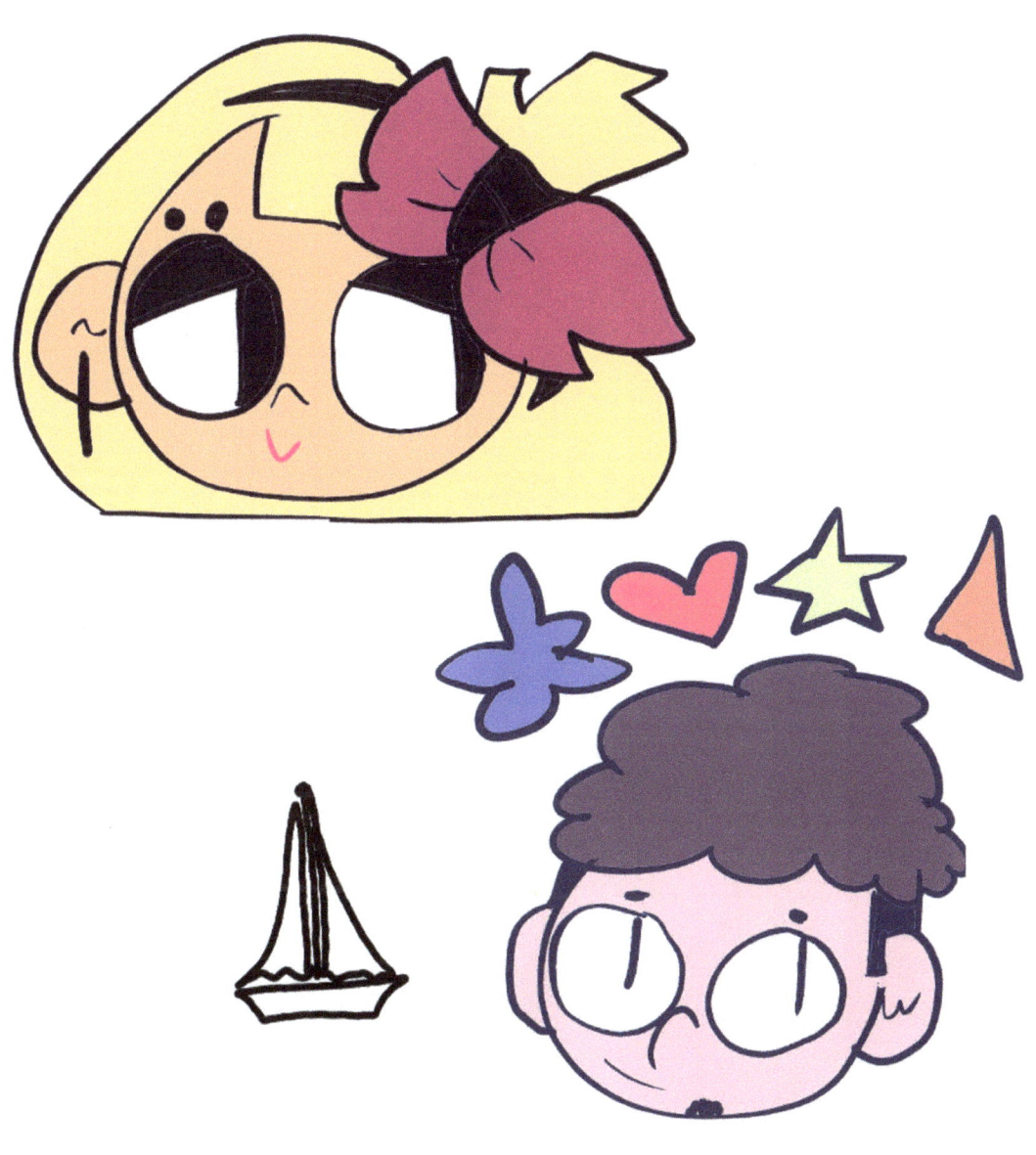

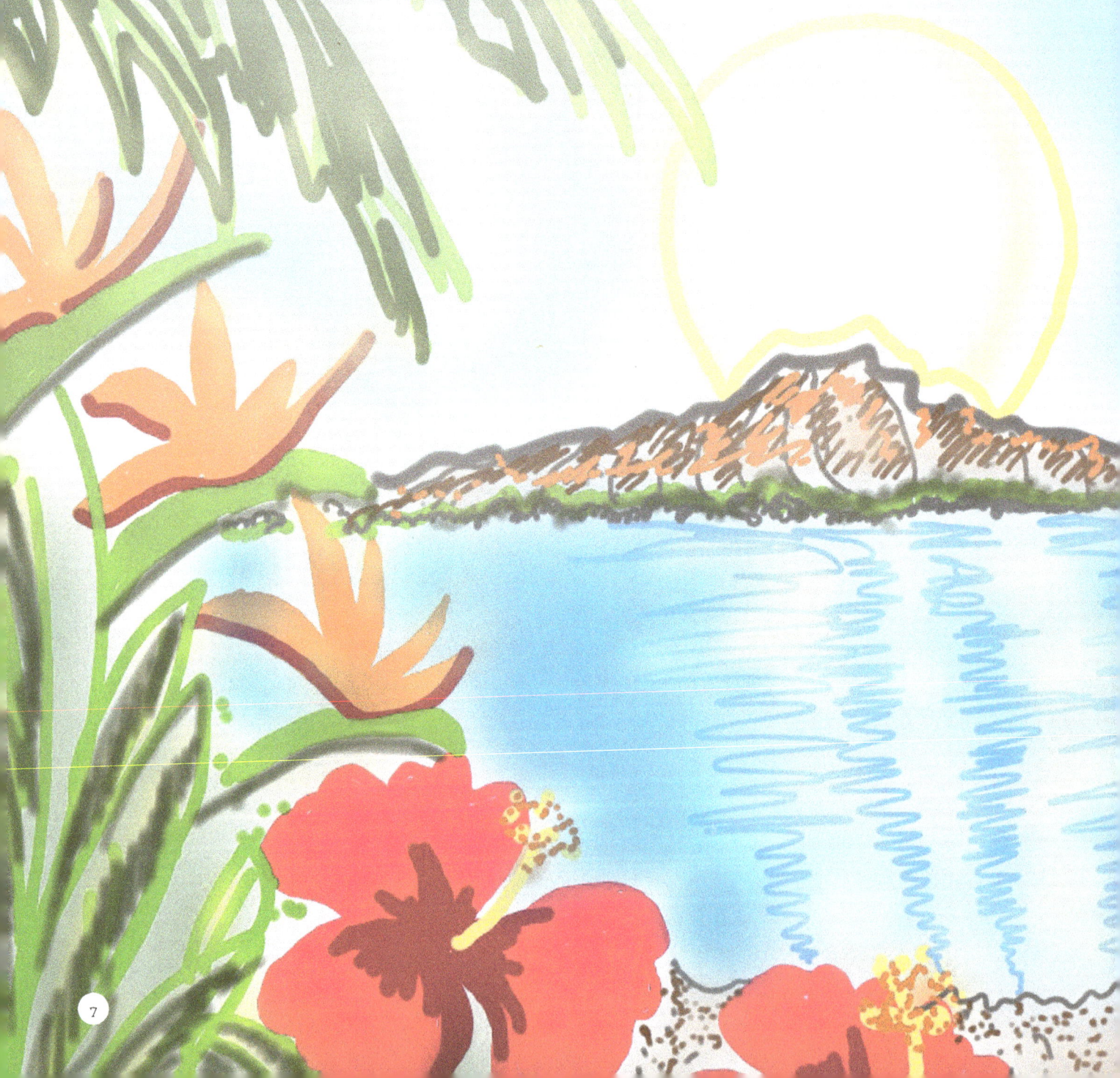

"Let's bring our picture to life," says Courageous Kate. "We need **color**!"
Super Joe began using the three primary colors, red, yellow and blue.
He mixed the primary colors and discovered three secondary colors,
purple, orange and green. "Just imagine," said Super Joe, "from the
primary and secondary colors, we can create six intermediate colors:
green-yellow, yellow-orange, orange-red, red-purple, purple-blue, and
blue-green. ...Awesome."

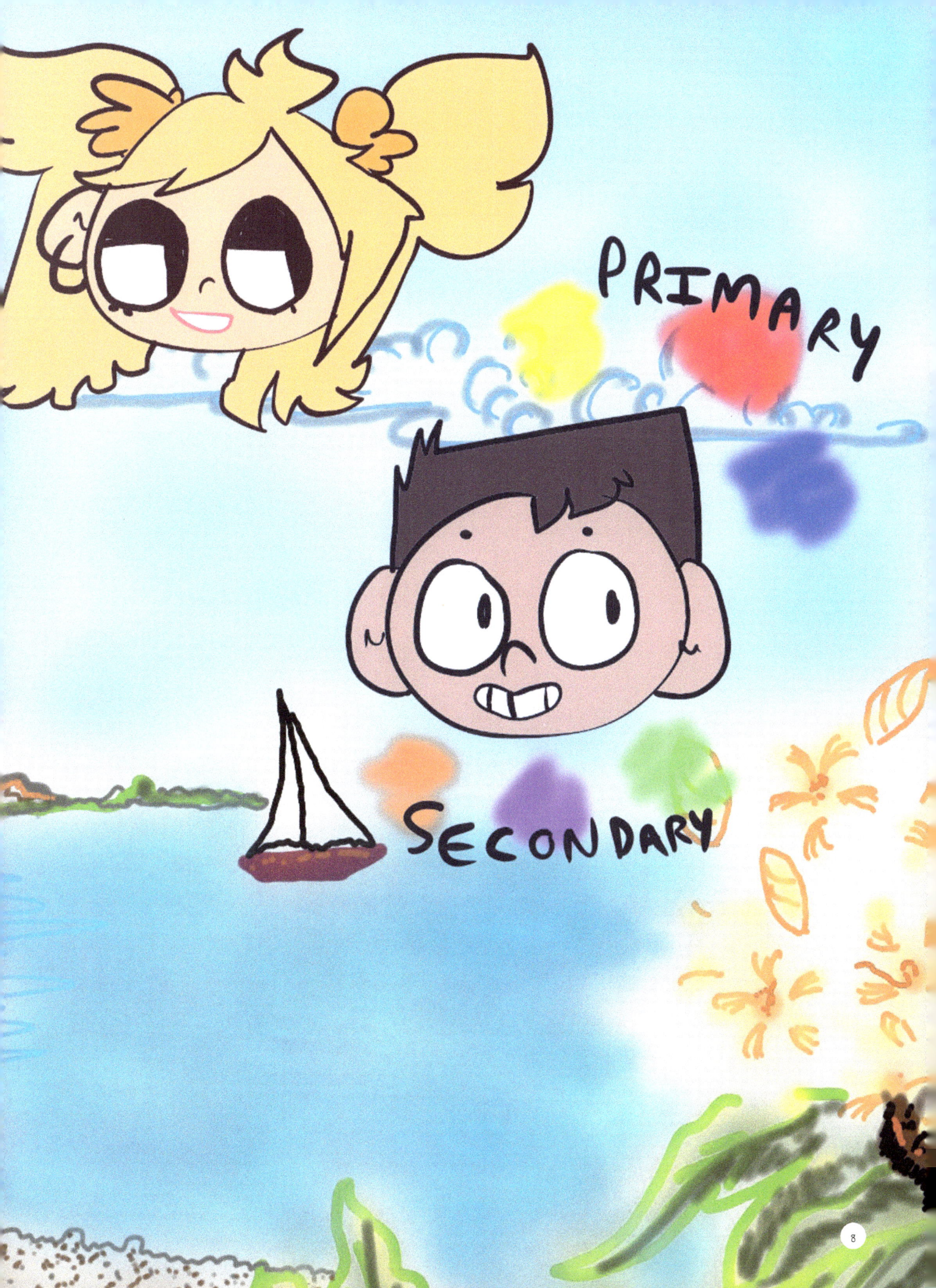

PRIMARY

SECONDARY

8

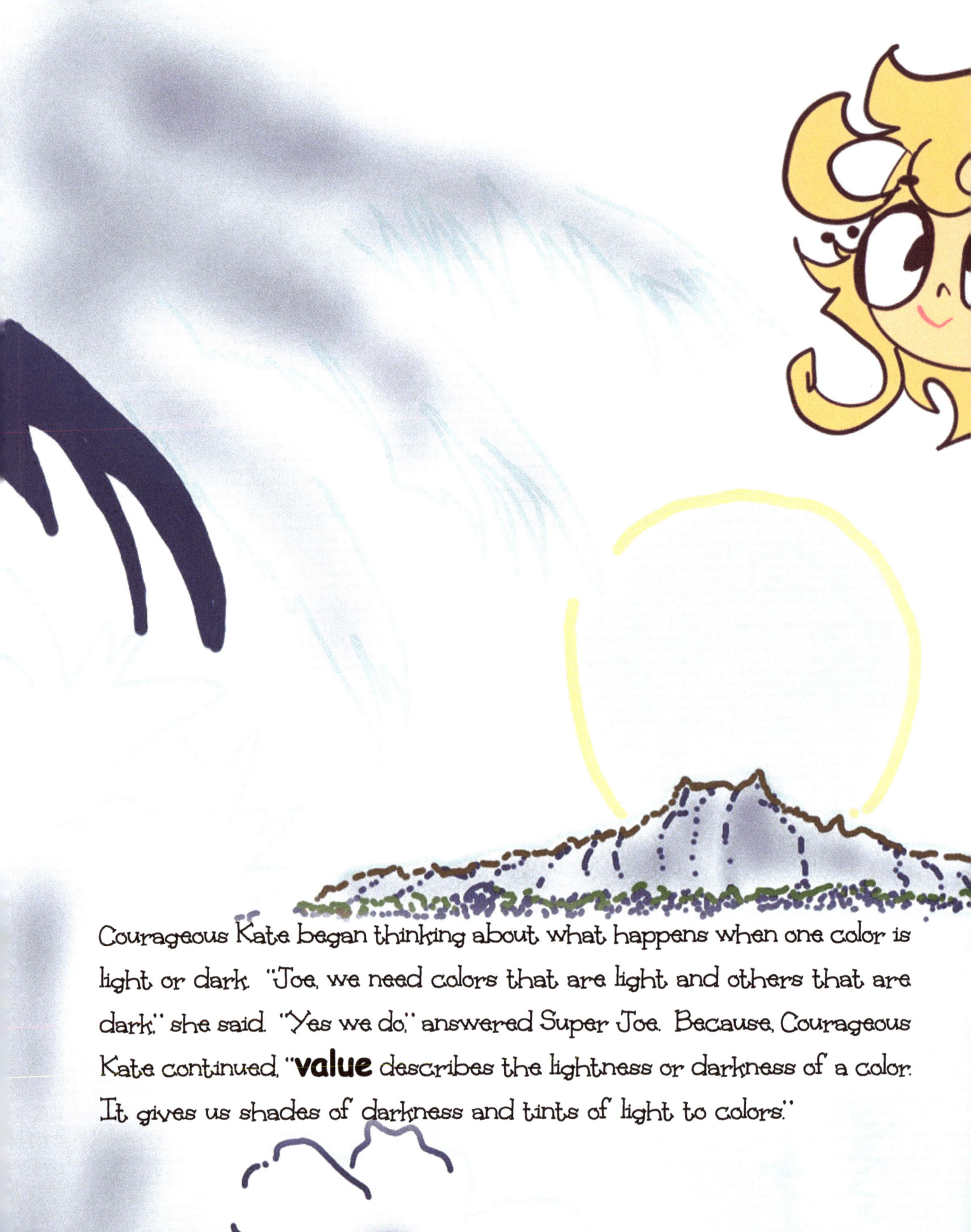

Courageous Kate began thinking about what happens when one color is light or dark. "Joe, we need colors that are light and others that are dark." she said. "Yes we do," answered Super Joe. Because, Courageous Kate continued, "**value** describes the lightness or darkness of a color. It gives us shades of darkness and tints of light to colors."

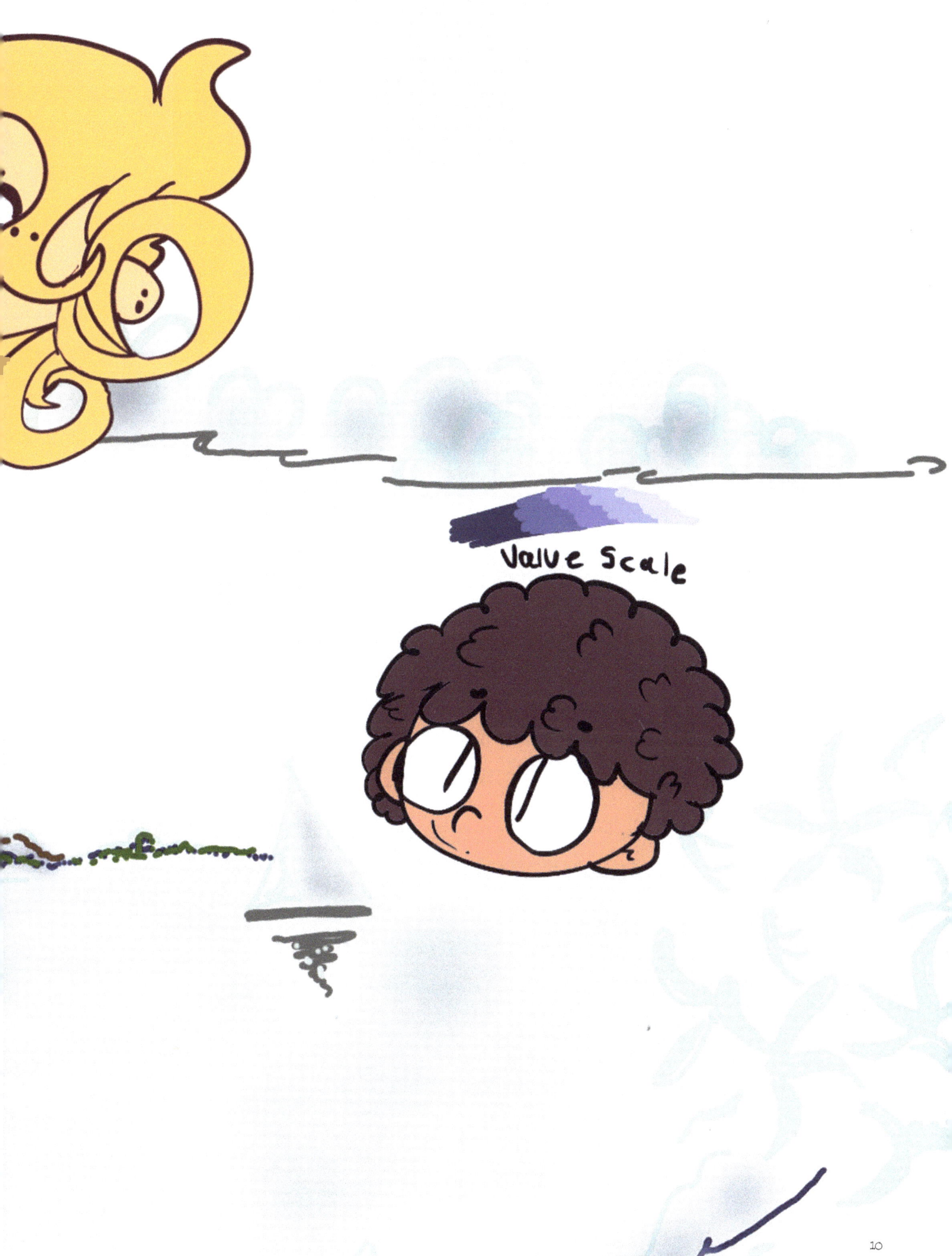

Value Scale

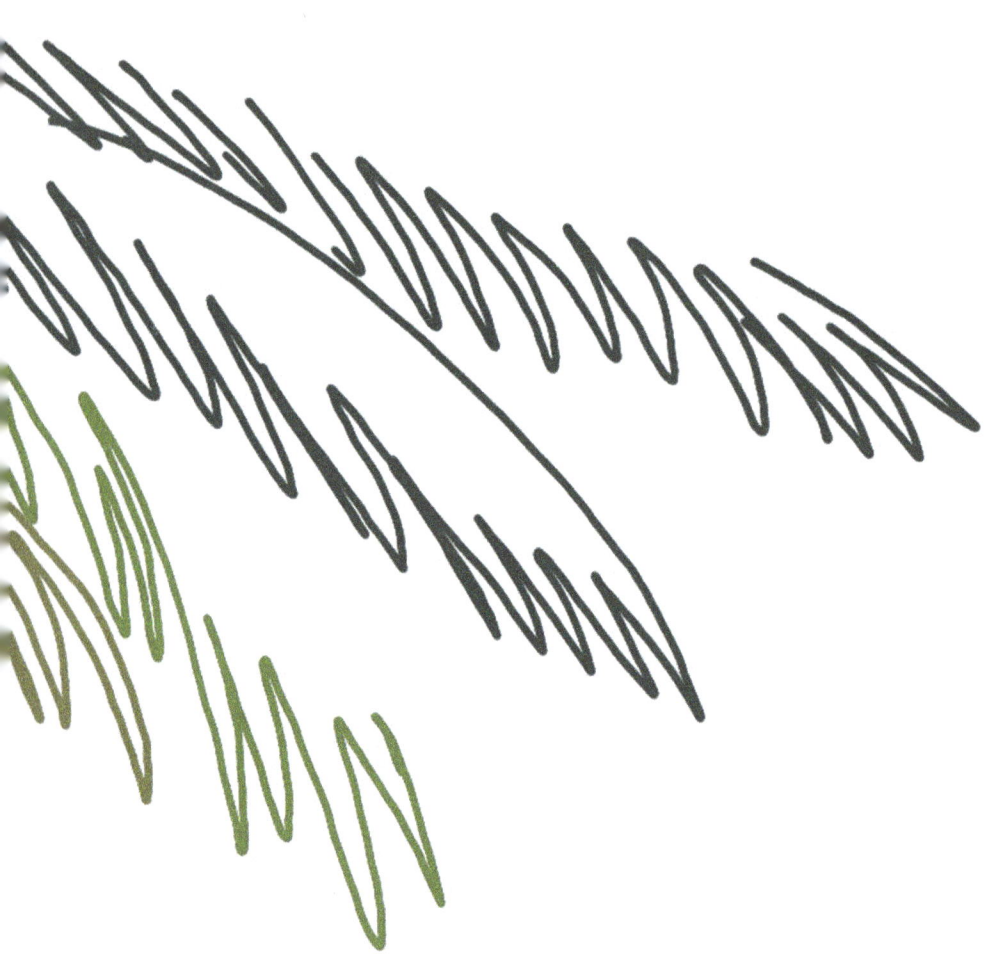

Courageous Kate sprung a new thought on Super Joe. "Joe, how do you think sand should feel, and trees and flowers? I think it's time to add **texture** to our picture so it can look like the way it really feels."

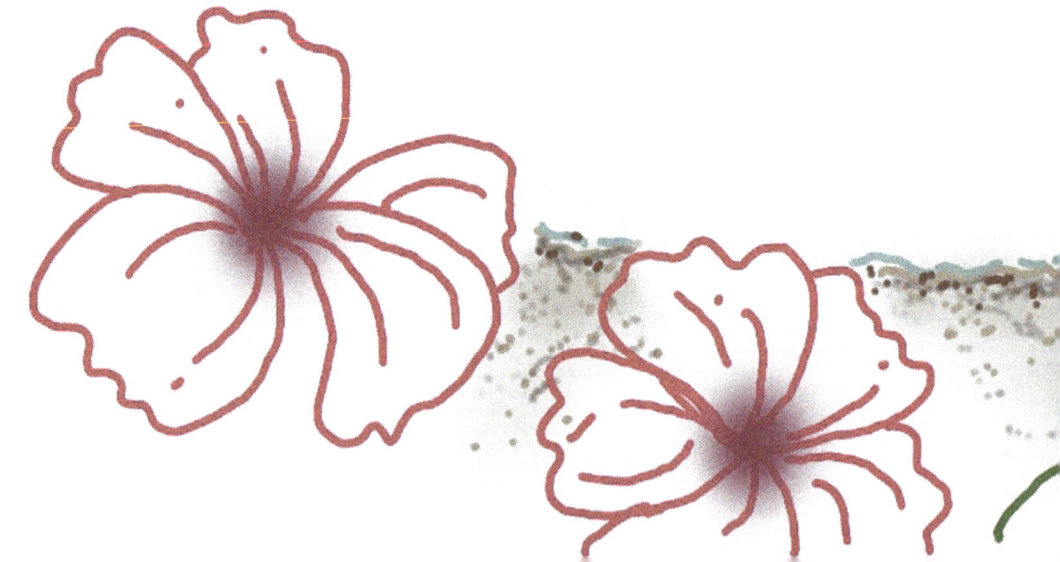

"By adding texture, we want to suggest that the sand is rough, flowers are soft and palm tree leaves are sharp," said Courageous Kate. Super Joe was intrigued and created texture by adding round bumps for sand, curved soft lines for flowers, and sharp pointed lines for palm tree leaves.

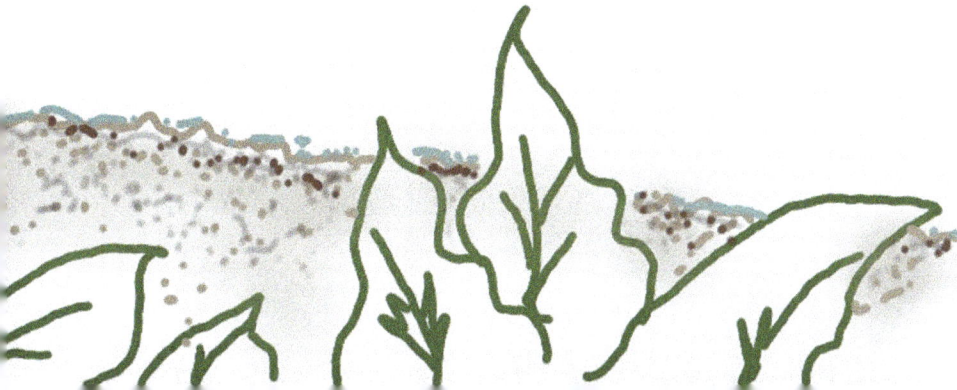

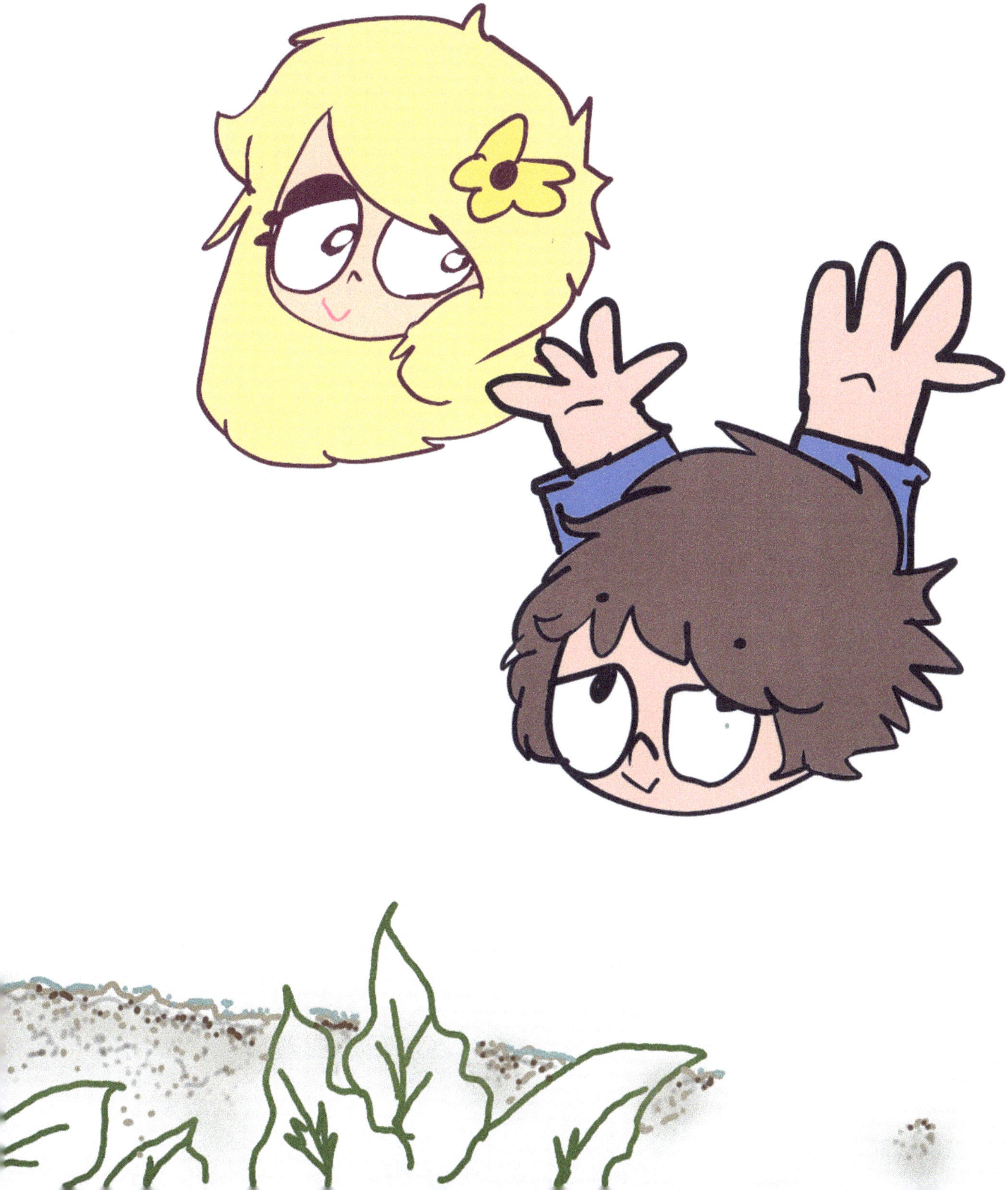

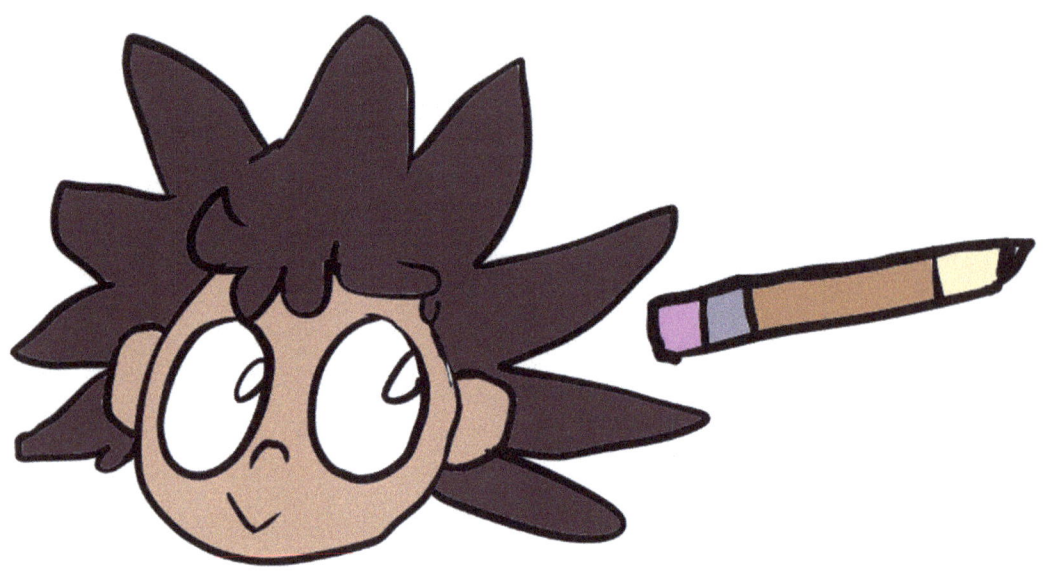

Super Joe went on to draw the island across the ocean that was in the background. Then he created flowers up front, in the foreground. "Wow!" said Courageous Kate. "The island looks so far away, but the flowers are so close up I think I can smell them."

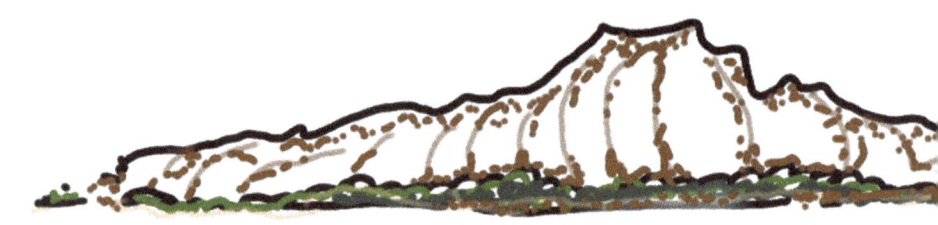

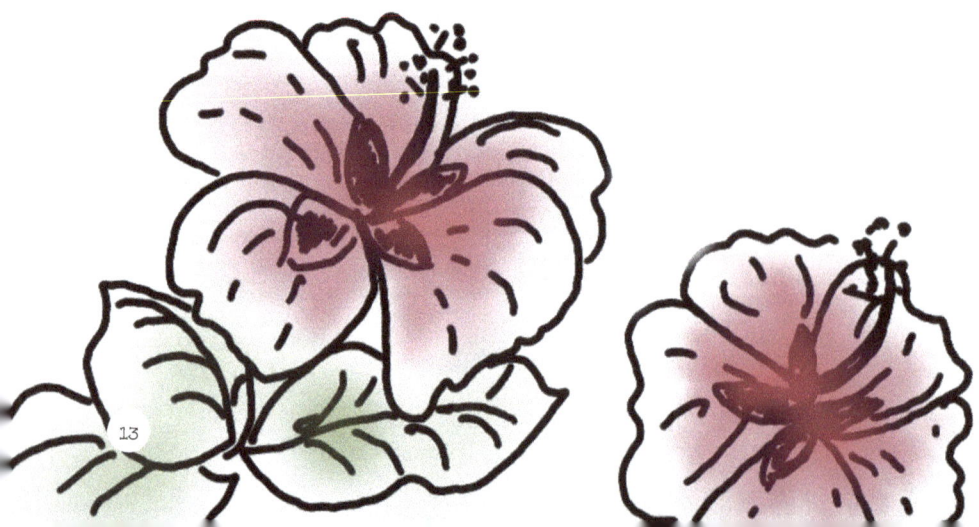

"Joe," said Courageous Kate, "you just created the illusion of **space**. The island looks distant because you made it so small — like it's far across the ocean, and the flowers look so close because you made them so large. That leaves the middle of the picture, which is called middle ground, where everything is medium size."

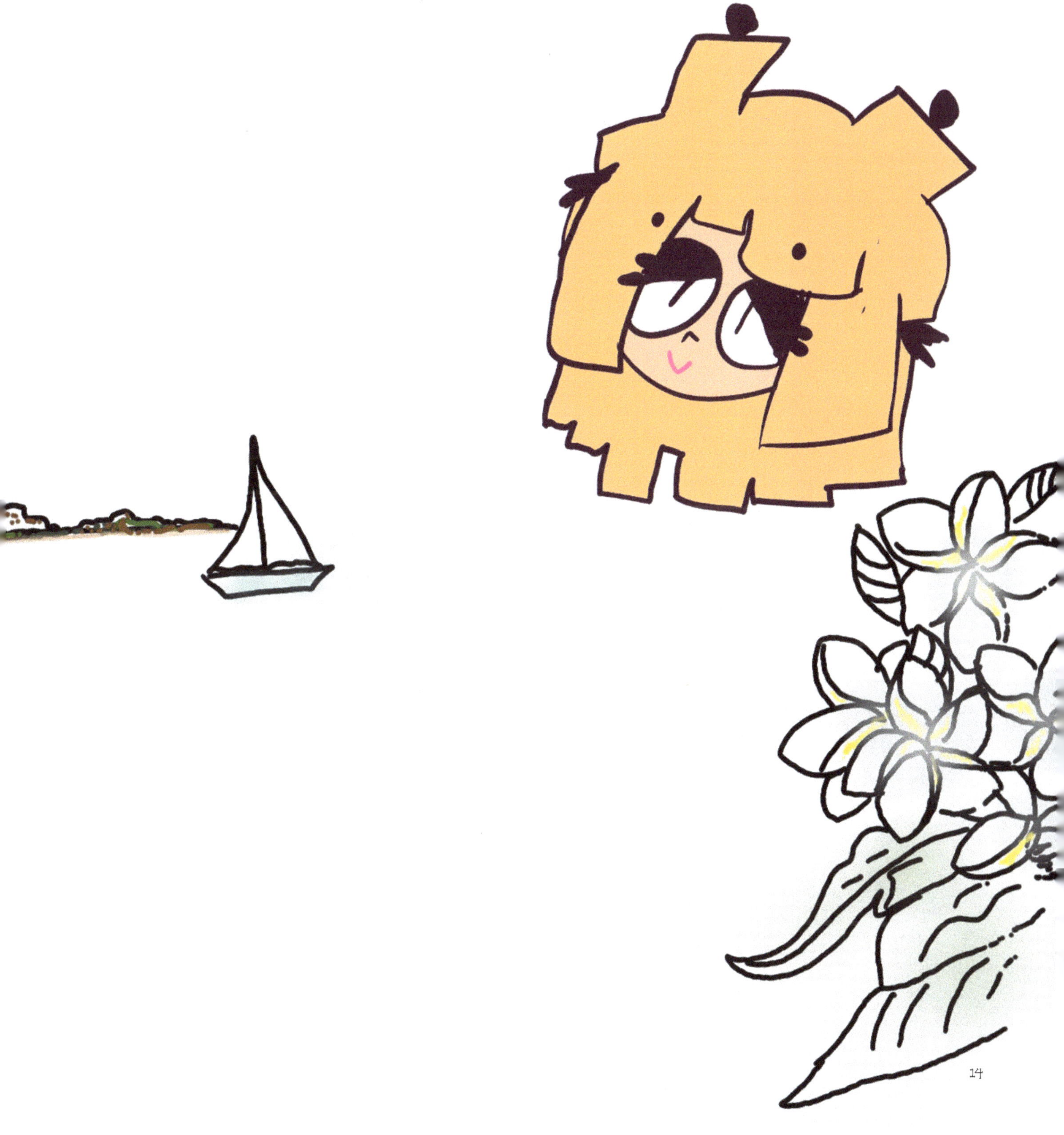

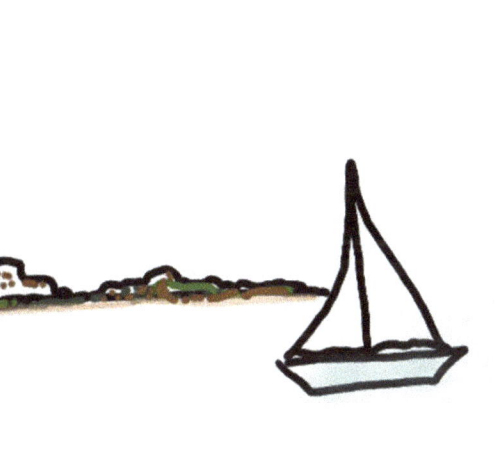

"And look at your island Joe, I can easily identify the top," said Courageous Kate. "The island must be round because I can see how the sides curve around. You used **form** to create the island so now we can identify the top and sides as they begin to wrap around to the other side. The island really looks real."

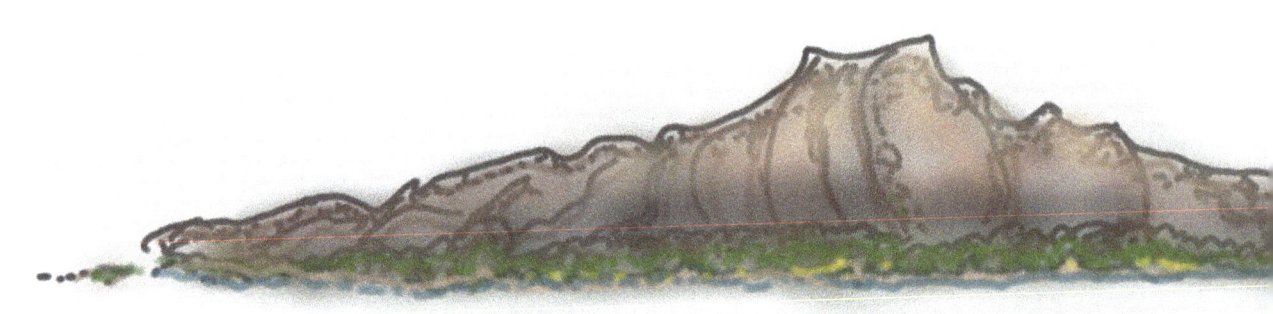

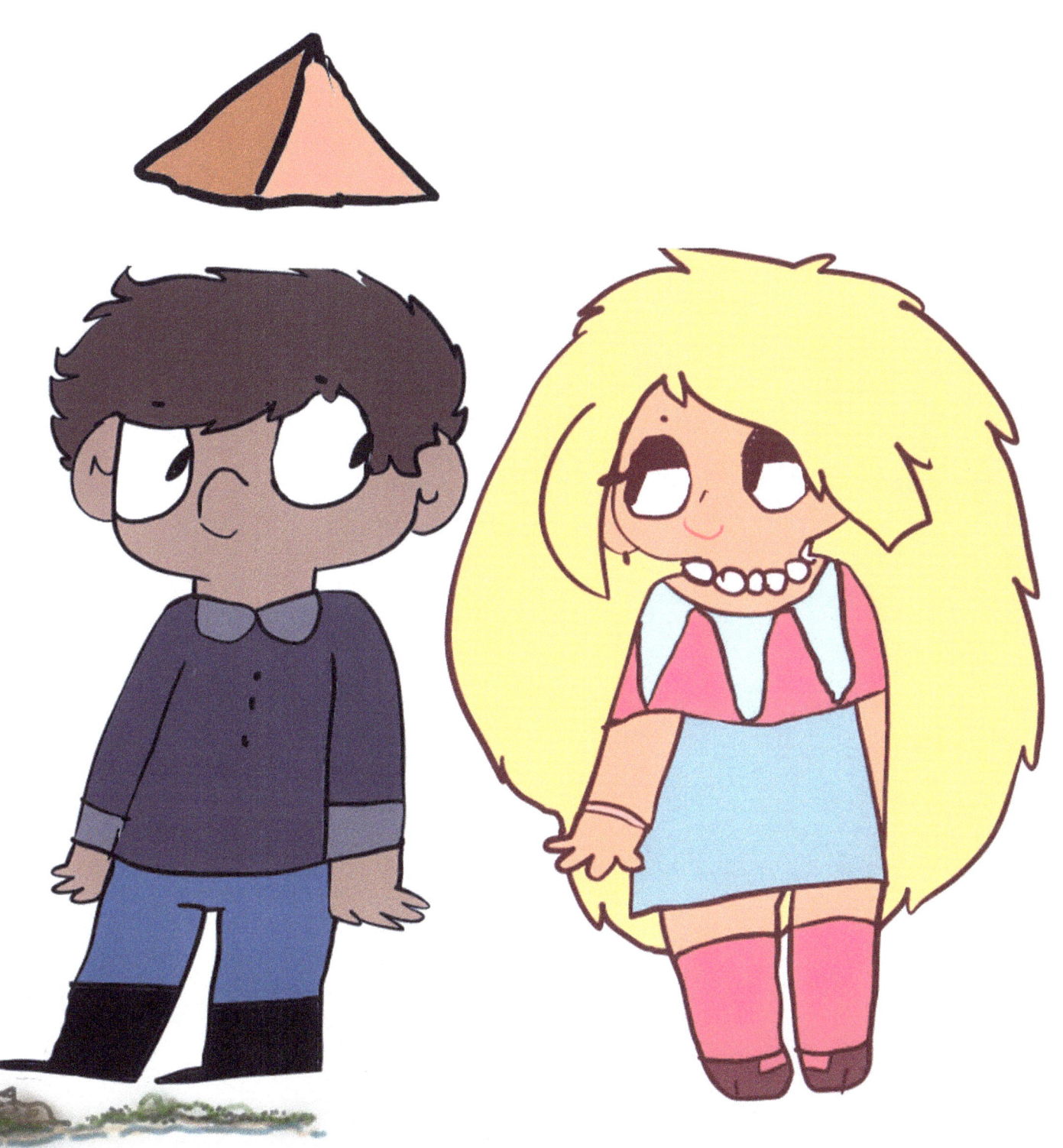

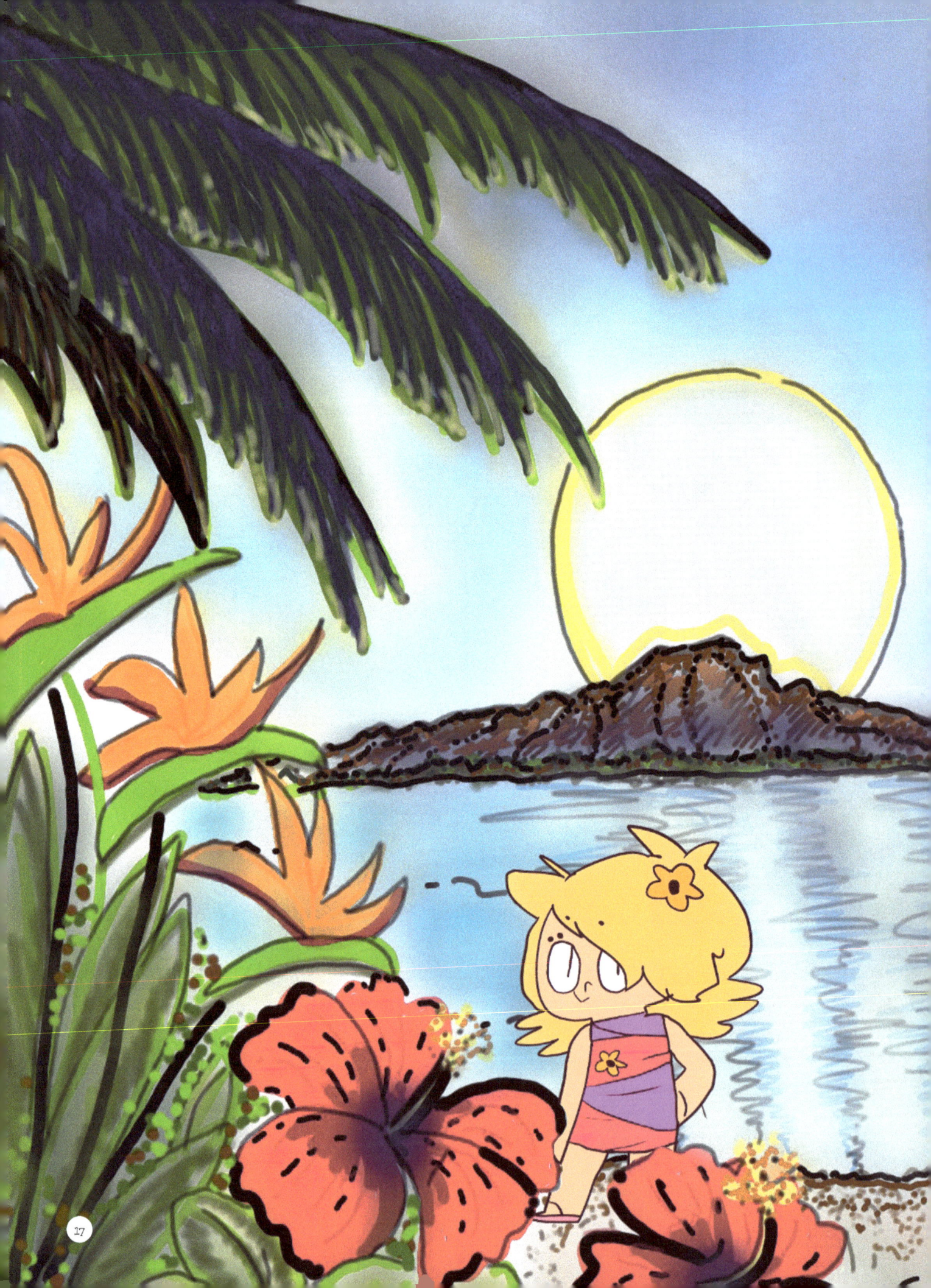

Super Joe was excited about their progress saying, "Let's see what happens when we put all seven elements together." "Yes!" answered Courageous Kate. "First we used **line**, then **shape, color, value, texture, space** and finally **form**! Joe, we created a complete picture of our favorite place at the beach just by using the seven elements of art." Super Joe exclaimed, "We sure did! All seven elements work together and are unified now; they're in **unity**." "Unity? What is unity," asked Courageous Kate. "Well Kate, that's another story for another time!" said Super Joe with a wink.

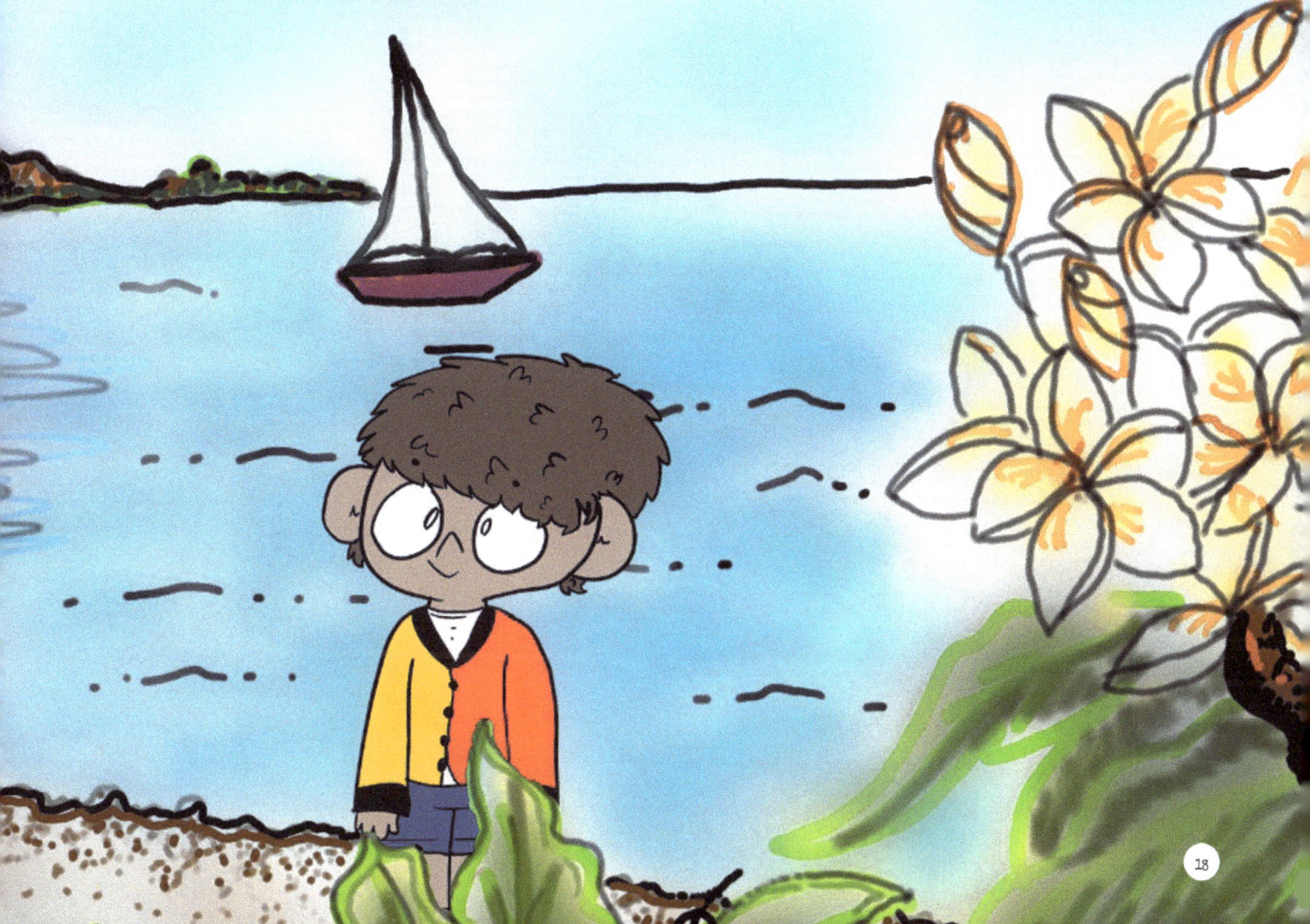

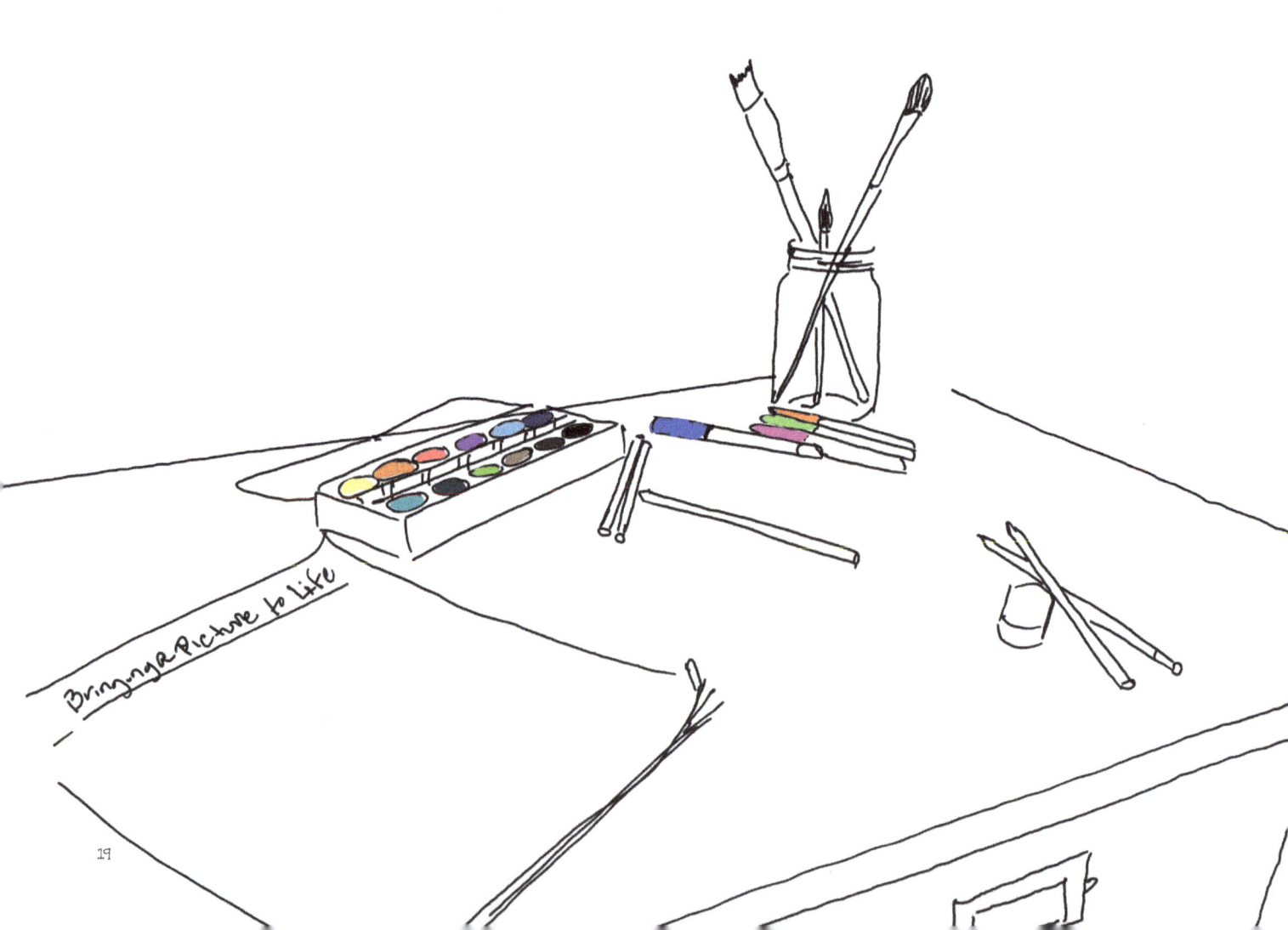

Bring-ing a Picture to Life

Let's review the seven elements, the building blocks of art.

Line
Shape
Color
Value
Texture
Space
Form

How can you use the seven elements in your art?

Let's create your journey, using the seven elements of art, **line, shape, color, value, texture, space** and **form**

Happy creating!

About the Author and Illustrators

A couple of years ago, Katie Madison was in treatment for breast cancer (double negative, HER2 positive). During this time away from teaching, on a sleepless night, the idea for an art book on the Elements of Art came to her heart. She took note and began writing this story with her students in mind, and what she needed as an art educator in the classroom. Providing her students with a working visual definition of the building blocks of art, her book demonstrates to each student how their art can be achieved skillfully and successfully.

Katie wrote this book to share with her students, yet all readers will enjoy learning how art can be expertly created. The response from students, family, and friends has been overwhelming positive. *Bringing a Picture to Life* became Katie's dream during a time of trial. To now live out her vision of inspiring students and to instill the love of creativity in each one of us, fills her with much joy.

While illustrating her book, Katie discovered that she needed help with the creation of Courageous Kate and Super Joe. Several years prior, Katie had the pleasure of teaching an eighth grade student, Giuliana, who had a very special gift for drawing characters. Reaching out to Giuliana and asking her to collaborate on the character drawings brings new life to each page. With a thankful and enthusiastic heart, Katie is pleased to introduce to you Giuliana.

When Katie is not teaching, she can be found searching for recipes, juicing, cooking in the kitchen with Joe, gardening, and embracing a new spiritual self and path. Katie, Joe and family live in Anthem, Arizona, with Duke, Cookie, Cali, Diesel, Pelly, Bubbles and Harmony.

Giuliana DeVivo is a happy 17-year-old high school student living in Anthem, Arizona with her family. She is very creative and artistic, loves drawing, music, animals and traveling.

She has a few challenges that she lives with. She was born with Albinism, which causes her to be visually impaired and diagnosed with Asperger's Syndrome at the age of 7, mostly due to her social anxiety. Giuliana does not allow these challenges to stop her from doing whatever she wants to do in her life.

About a year ago, her previous art teacher, Katie Madison, contacted her to help illustrate the characters in a book that she was writing called *Bringing a Picture to Life*. Giuliana was very excited for the opportunity to create something that could show the world her unique art style.

After graduating from high school, she plans on going to college for Special Education and will also receive her certification to train guide dogs.

She would like to thank Katie Madison for her kindness, patience and for this amazing opportunity.

Acknowledgements

This journey to wellness brought about a rebirth to life and to live purposefully. Looking back, I can see it now that God put me on this journey to teach me, to change the direction of my life, to give me purpose. With much gratefulness, I thank Joe, Zach and Maddie, my family, my dearest designers and church friends, my school colleagues, friends, students, doctors and nurses... you know who you are. Many thanks to all of the art educators, who have shaped the kind of teacher I have become, and aspire to be.

www.ingramcontent.com/pod-product-compliance
Lightning Source LLC
Chambersburg PA
CBHW052143170526

45159CB00017B/3143